JI[...] X

Pacific

Photography by SIMON WHEELER

THE MASTER CHEFS
WEIDENFELD & NICOLSON
LONDON

JILL DUPLEIX is one of Australia's leading cookery writers. She is the author of seven cookbooks, including *New Food*, which won the Australian Publishers Award for best-designed book of 1994, and *Allegro al dente*, a collection of pasta recipes accompanied by a CD of some of the world's best-loved opera arias. Both books have been published in the UK by Mitchell Beazley. She is also the food editor of *The Sydney Morning Herald* and *Elle Australia*, and is a popular food commentator on radio and television.

She lives on the edge of the Pacific Ocean in Sydney, Australia, where she draws inspiration from the tangy, tropical tastes of the foods of the Pacific Rim.

Photograph by Arunas

CONTENTS

Do not fuss with the

natural state of the

food just to show

you are a clever cook.

YUAN MEI

INTRODUCTION

The food of the Pacific is hot, tropical, fresh and fruity. It's as bright as a rainforest parrot, as invigorating as a squeeze of lime juice, as sweet as coconut milk, as tangy as pineapple and as fresh as a mahi mahi fish flapping on the buttery sand of a sun-drenched island.

This vibrant, sea-salty cuisine is drawn from the islands of Hawaii, Tahiti and Fiji, the shores of New Zealand, the dynamic new world cooking of Australia and, across the wide blue ocean, from Japan, Malaysia, Indonesia, Thailand and Vietnam.

The food of the Pacific is not East meets West, nor North meets South, but simply light, bright, healthy cooking, informed by European techniques and Asian flavours. It is always eaten in a simple, stylish manner that emphasizes fresh air and sunshine. In other words, it is delicious.

Jill Dupleix

PACIFIC OYSTERS
with lightly pickled vegetables

1 LARGE KNOB OF FRESH GINGER

1 CUCUMBER

1 CARROT

½ GIANT WHITE RADISH
(MOOLI/DAIKON)

250 ML/8 FL OZ WHITE RICE
VINEGAR

2 DOZEN FRESHLY OPENED PACIFIC
OYSTERS

2 TABLESPOONS FINELY SLICED
JAPANESE PICKLED GINGER

SERVES 4

Peel the ginger, cucumber, carrot and radish. Cut into 5 cm/2 inch lengths. Cut lengthways into thin slices, then cut the slices into very fine matchstick strips. Place the strips in a glass bowl, add the rice vinegar and leave in the refrigerator to marinate for at least 1 hour.

Loosen each oyster on its shell and divide the shells between four platters. Spoon a few of the marinated vegetables and their dressing on to each oyster. Top each oyster with a slice of pickled ginger and serve at once.

For a party, the oysters and their dressing can be served in small Chinese soup spoons, arranged on a tray.

TUNA WITH WASABI
on chicory

300 G/11 OZ VERY FRESH
  (NOT PREVIOUSLY FROZEN),
  TOP-QUALITY RAW TUNA
1 TEASPOON SMALL CAPERS, RINSED
  AND CHOPPED
1 TEASPOON CHOPPED GHERKINS
  (CORNICHON PICKLES)
2 ANCHOVY FILLETS, CHOPPED
2 SPRING ONIONS, FINELY CHOPPED
1 TABLESPOON VEGETABLE OIL
1 TEASPOON SOY SAUCE
1 EGG YOLK
1 TEASPOON WASABI (JAPANESE
  HORSERADISH) POWDER, MIXED
  WITH WATER TO FORM A PASTE
SALT AND FRESHLY GROUND BLACK
  PEPPER
4 LARGE HEADS OF CHICORY

MAKES 24 PIECES

Cut the tuna into very small dice.

In a bowl, mix the chopped capers, pickles, anchovies, spring onions, oil, soy sauce, egg yolk, wasabi paste and a little salt and pepper. Add the tuna and toss gently. Taste and adjust the seasoning if required.

Cut off the chicory roots and carefully pull the leaves apart. Wash the leaves and pat dry with paper towels. Arrange on platters, like the spokes of a wheel. To serve, spoon the marinated tuna mixture into the hollow base of each leaf.

Instead of chicory, the tuna mixture can also be served in small leaves of Cos lettuce.

RAW FISH WITH LIME,

coconut and avocado

400 G/14 OZ VERY FRESH
   DEEP SEA FISH
5 TABLESPOONS FRESH LIME JUICE
1 SCANT TEASPOON SALT
250 ML/8 FL OZ CANNED
   COCONUT MILK
1 AVOCADO
4 TOMATOES, SKINNED, SEEDED AND
   DICED
1 CUCUMBER, PEELED AND DICED
2 TABLESPOONS FRESH CORIANDER
   LEAVES

SERVES 4

Cut the fish into bite-size pieces or thin slices. Place in a glass bowl, add 4 tablespoons of the lime juice and the salt and leave in the refrigerator to marinate for at least 3 hours, tossing occasionally.

Add the coconut milk and gently mix with the fish.

Peel the avocado, cut into cubes and sprinkle with the remaining lime juice.

Drain the fish and gently toss with the avocado, tomatoes, cucumber and coriander. Divide between four cocktail glasses or serve in a hollowed-out coconut.

RICE PAPER ROLLS
with prawns and mint

ABOUT 50 G/2 OZ CELLOPHANE
NOODLES (RICE VERMICELLI)
12 DRIED RICE PAPER ROUNDS
(BANH TRANG), ABOUT 22 CM/
9 INCHES IN DIAMETER
ABOUT ½ SMALL ICEBERG LETTUCE,
SHREDDED
50 G/2 OZ FRESH BEANSPROUTS,
RINSED
3 TABLESPOONS SALTED PEANUTS
HANDFUL OF FRESH MINT
HANDFUL OF FRESH CORIANDER
12 SMALL PRAWNS, LIGHTLY
COOKED AND PEELED

TO SERVE

SWEET CHILLI SAUCE (PAGE 29),
FOR DIPPING

MAKES 12

Cook the noodles in boiling water for 2 minutes or until tender. Drain and rinse in cold water, then drain again.

Dunk a rice paper round into simmering water for a few seconds until soft, then lay on a serving plate. Top with some shredded lettuce, noodles, beansprouts, nuts, mint and coriander leaves, and fold the rice paper towards the centre to form a firm roll.

Tuck in one small prawn, fold in the ends of the roll, and continue to roll into a neat sausage shape. The rice paper will stick to itself and hold the shape. Continue with the remaining rice paper rounds. Dip into the sauce and eat with the fingers.

CURRY PUFFS

with peanut sambal

1 TABLESPOON CURRY POWDER

½ TEASPOON PAPRIKA

2 TABLESPOONS PEANUT OIL

125 G/4 OZ PUMPKIN, PEELED AND
CUT INTO SMALL DICE

1 POTATO, PAR-BOILED AND CUT
INTO SMALL DICE

1 SMALL CARROT, CHOPPED

1 ONION, CHOPPED

50 G/2 OZ COOKED PEAS

PINCH OF SUGAR

½ TEASPOON SALT

175 G/6 OZ PUFF PASTRY

VEGETABLE OIL FOR DEEP-FRYING

TO SERVE

PEANUT SAMBAL (PAGE 28)

MAKES 10

Mix the curry powder and paprika
together with a little water to form
a paste.

Heat a wok, add the oil and,
when hot, add the curry paste and
stir-fry for 2 minutes. Add the
vegetables and stir-fry for a further
2 minutes.

Add 125 ml/4 fl oz water,
cover and cook over a gentle heat
until the vegetables are cooked, soft
and dry. Stir in the sugar and salt
and leave to cool.

Roll out the pastry to about
2 mm/¹⁄₁₆ inch thick. Cut out ten
circles, about 10 cm/4 inches in
diameter, using a small saucer or
Chinese bowl as a guide. Place a
spoonful of filling in the centre of
each pastry circle.

Moisten the edges with water
and fold the pastry over to form a
plump half moon shape, pressing
the edges together to seal. Take a
small section at the top of the
curve between thumb and
forefinger, pinch it, pull it slightly,
then fold it back on to the curry
puff. Repeat until you have an
attractive crimped edge.

In a wok, heat the oil for deep-
frying to 180–190°C/350–375°F
or until a cube of bread browns in
30 seconds. Deep-fry the curry
puffs until golden, then drain on
paper towels. Serve warm, with
peanut sambal.

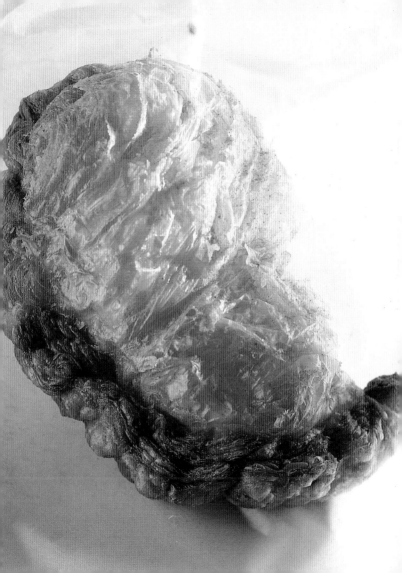

SOBA NOODLES
with chicken and ginger

500 G/1¼ LB DRIED SOBA
(BUCKWHEAT) NOODLES
1 TABLESPOON SESAME OIL
1 WHOLE CHICKEN, POACHED OR
STEAMED
1 CUCUMBER
1 TABLESPOON FRESH CORIANDER
LEAVES

DRESSING
BUNCH OF SPRING ONIONS
8 TABLESPOONS FRESH (UNUSED)
PEANUT OIL
2 TABLESPOONS SHREDDED FRESH
GINGER
1 TEASPOON SALT

SERVES 4

Cook the noodles in boiling water
for a few minutes, separating them
carefully, until tender but still firm.
Drain, refresh in cold water, drain
again and toss in sesame oil. Chill
until ready to serve.

Shred the chicken, discarding
the bones and most of the skin; do
not chill or it will numb the flavour.

Peel the cucumber, cut in half
lengthways, scoop out the seeds
with a teaspoon and cut the flesh
into matchstick strips.

For the dressing, finely chop the
green stems of the spring onions.
Gently warm the peanut oil in a
small saucepan with the ginger and
salt, stirring until the salt dissolves.
Add the spring onions and stir for a
few seconds until they wilt and
soften, then remove from the heat.

In a bowl, combine the
shredded chicken, cucumber,
noodles, coriander and half the
warm dressing; toss gently. To serve,
twirl the noodles on a large fork
and arrange in a pyramid in the
centre of each plate. Top each
pyramid with a spoonful of the
remaining spring onion dressing.

HOT AND SOUR BEEF SALAD

300 G/11 OZ FILLET STEAK
1 TEASPOON FISH SAUCE

DRESSING

2 TABLESPOONS UNCOOKED
   JASMINE RICE
2 DRIED RED CHILLIES (OR
   ½ TEASPOON CHILLI POWDER)
4 RED SHALLOTS, FINELY SLICED
LARGE HANDFUL OF FRESH MINT
   LEAVES
SMALL HANDFUL OF FRESH
   CORIANDER LEAVES
2 SPRING ONIONS, FINELY SLICED
2 TABLESPOONS LIME JUICE
2 TABLESPOONS FISH SAUCE
½ TEASPOON SUGAR

**SERVES 2 FOR LUNCH,
4 AS PART OF A THAI MEAL**

Heat a heavy-bottomed frying pan, add the rice and toast over medium heat until golden. Grind or pound the rice to a powder and set aside. Reheat the frying pan and add the dried chillies. Toast until smoky, then grind or pound to a powder and set aside.

Grill or pan-sear the steak quickly, leaving it quite rare. Sprinkle with the fish sauce and leave to rest for 10 minutes.

Mix ½ teaspoon of the ground roasted chilli powder (store the rest) and the rice powder with the shallots, mint, coriander, spring onions, lime juice, fish sauce and sugar. Taste and adjust the seasoning if required: it should be hot, sour and salty.

Slice the beef thinly and toss through the salad, together with any juices. Pile high on a plate and serve at once.

As a simple lunch, it can be accompanied by a platter of crunchy lettuces and cucumber.

MACADAMIA NUT TART

SHORTCRUST PASTRY (PAGE 30)
300 G/11 OZ MACADAMIA NUTS
4 EGGS
225 G/8 OZ SOFT BROWN SUGAR
175 ML/6 FL OZ LIGHT CORN
   SYRUP (LIQUID GLUCOSE)
3 TABLESPOONS MELTED BUTTER
1 TEASPOON VANILLA ESSENCE

SERVES 8

Roll out the pastry to about
3 mm/⅛ inch thick and use to line
a buttered 25 cm/10 inch round
flan tin. Place in the refrigerator
and chill for 30 minutes.

Preheat the oven to 180°C/
350°F/Gas Mark 4. Prick the base
of the pastry, line with a circle of
greaseproof paper and fill with
baking beans. Bake for about
12–15 minutes or until the pastry
is almost cooked but not browned.

Discard the paper and baking
beans and fill the pastry case with
macadamia nuts. Increase the oven
temperature to 200°C /400°F/Gas
Mark 6.

Beat the eggs and add the
sugar, corn syrup, butter and
vanilla. Mix well, then pour over
the nuts and bake for 10 minutes.

Reduce the oven temperature
to 180°C/350°F/Gas Mark 4 and
bake for 40 minutes or until
completely set. If the edge of the
pastry edge is browning too
quickly, cover it with foil. Leave in
the oven to cool completely before
serving, which will help it to
become firm.

TROPICAL FRUIT SOUP
with lemongrass

RIND OF 1 ORANGE, CUT INTO
    TINY STRIPS
RIND OF 1 LEMON, CUT INTO TINY
    STRIPS
1 BOTTLE (75 CL) WHITE DESSERT
    WINE
2 TABLESPOONS CASTER SUGAR
1 VANILLA POD, SPLIT LENGTHWAYS
1 TABLESPOON GRATED FRESH
    GINGER
2 STALKS OF FRESH LEMONGRASS
5 CLOVES
SMALL BUNCH OF FRESH MINT
    LEAVES
4 PASSIONFRUIT
450 G/1 LB (PEELED WEIGHT)
    MIXED TROPICAL FRUIT
    (PINEAPPLE, MANGO, PEACH,
    PAPAYA, KIWI FRUIT, LYCHEES,
    BANANA), PEELED AND CUBED
150 G/5 OZ STRAWBERRIES AND
    OTHER BERRIES IN SEASON
FRESH MINT LEAVES, TO DECORATE

SERVES 4

Place the orange and lemon rind, wine, sugar, vanilla pod, ginger, lemongrass, cloves and mint leaves in a saucepan and add 500 ml/16 fl oz cold water. Bring to the boil and simmer for 30 minutes.

Cover the pan, leave to cool, then chill overnight.

The next day, strain the syrup through a fine sieve, reserving the lemongrass and the orange and lemon rind.

Cut the passionfruit in half, scoop out the pulp and push it through a sieve. Add the passionfruit juice to the syrup.

Prepare the fruit and berries and arrange in four chilled soup plates, tucking extra mint leaves among the fruit. Spoon the syrup over the fruit until it just starts to float. Serve sprinkled with a few pieces of the reserved lemongrass and orange and lemon rind.

THE BASICS

PEANUT SAMBAL

- 1 ONION OR 6 SHALLOTS, GRATED
- 2 GARLIC CLOVES, CRUSHED
- 3 CANDLENUTS OR MACADAMIA
  NUTS, CRUSHED
- 2 STALKS OF LEMONGRASS, WHITE
  PART ONLY, FLATTENED
- 2 DRIED RED CHILLIES, SOAKED,
  DRAINED AND CHOPPED
- 4 TABLESPOONS PEANUT OIL
- 1 TEASPOON GROUND CORIANDER
- 1 TEASPOON GROUND TURMERIC
- 375 ML/12 FL OZ COCONUT MILK
- 1 TEASPOON TAMARIND SOAKED IN
  3 TABLESPOONS WATER
- 1 TABLESPOON SUGAR
- 1 TEASPOON SALT
- 125 G/4 OZ PEANUTS, ROUGHLY
  CHOPPED

Pound or blend together the onion, garlic, candlenuts or macadamias, lemongrass and chillies to form a paste.

Heat the oil in a wok or saucepan over a low heat and cook the paste for a few minutes, until it smells fragrant.

Stir in the coriander and turmeric. Add the coconut milk and heat gently, stirring. Add the tamarind water, sugar, salt and peanuts and simmer for 2 minutes. Leave to cool to room temperature before serving.

This can be made in advance and frozen.

SWEET CHILLI SAUCE

2 TABLESPOONS SUGAR
1 GARLIC CLOVE, CRUSHED
2 TABLESPOONS FISH SAUCE
2 TABLESPOONS FRESH LIME OR
   LEMON JUICE
1 SMALL FRESH RED CHILLI, SLICED
1 TABLESPOON WHITE WINE
   VINEGAR OR RICE VINEGAR
1 SLICE OF LIME OR LEMON

Dissolve the sugar in 2 tablespoons boiling water.

Stir in the crushed garlic, fish sauce, lime or lemon juice, chilli and vinegar. Cut the slice of lime or lemon into tiny wedges and float on top of the sauce.

SHORTCRUST PASTRY

150 G/5 OZ BUTTER
275 G/10 OZ PLAIN FLOUR
CHILLED WATER

Chop the butter into small pieces and place in a food processor with the flour.

Process until the mixture resembles sand. With the motor running, add chilled water, drop by drop, until the mixture forms a soft dough.

Wrap the dough in clingfilm and chill in the refrigerator for 30 minutes. Roll out on a lightly floured work surface.

THE MASTER CHEFS

SOUPS
ARABELLA BOXER

MEZE, TAPAS AND ANTIPASTI
AGLAIA KREMEZI

PASTA SAUCES
GORDON RAMSAY

RISOTTO
MICHELE SCICOLONE

SALADS
CLARE CONNERY

MEDITERRANEAN
ANTONY WORRALL THOMPSON

VEGETABLES
PAUL GAYLER

LUNCHES
ALASTAIR LITTLE

COOKING FOR TWO
RICHARD OLNEY

FISH
RICK STEIN

CHICKEN
BRUNO LOUBET

SUPPERS
VALENTINA HARRIS

THE MAIN COURSE
ROGER VERGÉ

ROASTS
JANEEN SARLIN

WILD FOOD
ROWLEY LEIGH

PACIFIC
JILL DUPLEIX

CURRIES
PAT CHAPMAN

HOT AND SPICY
PAUL AND JEANNE RANKIN

THAI
JACKI PASSMORE

CHINESE
YAN-KIT SO

VEGETARIAN
KAREN LEE

DESSERTS
MICHEL ROUX

CAKES
CAROLE WALTER

COOKIES
ELINOR KLIVANS

THE MASTER CHEFS

Text © copyright 1996 Jill Dupleix

Jill Dupleix has asserted her right to be
identified as the Author of this Work.

Photographs © copyright 1996 Simon Wheeler

First published in 1996 by
WEIDENFELD & NICOLSON
THE ORION PUBLISHING GROUP
ORION HOUSE
5 UPPER ST MARTIN'S LANE
LONDON WC2H 9EA

British Library Cataloguing-in-Publication data
A catalogue record for this book is available
from the British Library.

ISBN 0 297 83641 2

DESIGNED BY THE SENATE
EDITOR MAGGIE RAMSAY
FOOD STYLIST JOY DAVIES
ASSISTANT KATY HOLDER